A Child's View of a Prairie

by

Susan C. McDermott

AuthorHouse™
1663 Liberty Drive
Bloomington, IN 47403
www.authorhouse.com
Phone: 1 (800) 839-8640

Because of the dynamic nature of the Internet, any web addresses or links contained in this book may have changed
since publication and may no longer be valid. The views expressed in this work are solely those of the author and do
not necessarily reflect the views of the publisher, and the publisher hereby disclaims any responsibility for them.

This book is printed on acid-free paper.

ISBN: 978-1-4343-6191-2 (sc)
ISBN: 978-1-7283-2400-5 (e)

Library of Congress Control Number: 2008903966

Print information available on the last page.

Published by AuthorHouse 09/20/2019

authorHOUSE®

Dedication:

To my sons, David and Michael Cummings. I am proud of you.

Love, Mom

To my grandchildren – Kyle, Karis, Kaia and Ian

I love you, Grandma

Acknowledgements:

A special thank you to my husband John, mother Ilse, father Helmuth, daughters Jamie and Jessica for all their encouragement.

"Hello, I am Dave and this is my younger brother Mike sitting to the left of me. Welcome to a Wisconsin prairie. This is a different world with many interesting things to see."

"Here we see Mike standing in a prairie. Plants on the prairie range from small to very tall. There are also many insects that live on the prairie."

Prairies are full of wildflowers and grasses; there are no trees or bushes. Prairie plants bloom at different times from spring through fall. The prairie flowers and grasses are shorter in spring, taller in summer, and get up to ten feet tall in fall.

"Exploring can be fun, Mike. Let's get going!"

"Dave, look at all the **black-eyed Susan**. There are so many of them. They are pretty flowers with a funny name."

Black-eyed Susan will grow well in flower gardens. They grow one to three feet tall.

A ***black-eyed Susan*** has yellow petals around a brown center. The leaves and stems are green and hairy.

"Mike, can you see the grasshopper sitting on that flower?"

"Dave, look at the *yellow coneflower.* It looks like a black-eyed Susan, but it is different."

The **yellow coneflower** has a tall brown center and droopy yellow petals. It is on a long green stem with jagged leaves. It is sometimes called prairie coneflower. It grows eighteen inches to five feet tall.

"Look Dave, I see a dragonfly. See how the wings sparkle in the sun."

Many dragonflies make their home on the prairie.

"Mike, come look at these purple flowers. Mom told me this plant is **_purple prairie clover_**."

"See how the many little purple flowers open up from the bottom of the flower head to the top. The flower head looks like it has purple fringe around it."

The **purple prairie clover** flowers are on tall stems with little, narrow leaves. Native Americans crushed the leaves in water and put them on cuts or wounds. They grow one to three feet tall.

"Mike, I see a ladybug on this yellow flower. I heard mom say that this plant is called **hoary puccoon**. That sure is a strange name. I suppose since the prairie is so different the names of the flowers are too."

The yellow flowers are trumpet-like with five petals, and the leaves are green-gray and narrow. They grow eight to twelve inches tall.

"Dave, are these flowers *prairie blazing stars*? Look how tall they are. They are as tall as me."

"Look at all the tiny purple flowers that make up one long flower head."

The flower is on a tall stem with many thin leaves. The monarch butterfly loves drinking nectar from these flowers. They grow two to four feet tall.

"Dave, Mom says there are many different types of blazing stars. This ***prairie blazing star*** has white flowers."

There are also rough blazing stars on the prairie.

"Hey, Mike, let's stand behind this plant. Mom taught us this flower is called *prairie dock*. It sure is tall! Look how big the leaves are at the base of the plant."

"That's right, Dave. The leaves look like big arrowheads and the bright yellow flowers are on very tall stems."

The flowers have many thin petals. They grow five to seven feet tall.

"Let's touch the leaves. The leaves feel smooth on the front but rough on the back. Why do the leaves feel cold?"

"Mike, Mom says that it is because the tap root goes deep in the ground and brings up cold water to the leaves."

"Wow, look at all the plants we have seen. Can you pick out the *yellow coneflower*, *prairie blazing star*, and *prairie dock* leaf that we are looking at?"

"Dave, these flowers are tall too. They look like prairie dock, but the leaves are different."

The leaves are green and jagged.

"What do you think this is?"

"This plant is named **compassplant**."

"Dave, do you think the plant gives directions?"

"Yes, it does, Mike. The leaves of the **compassplant** seem to always go in a north-south direction."

The yellow daisy-like flowers are on a very tall stem. Like the prairie dock, the **compassplant** also has a tap root that goes deep into the ground. They grow three to nine feet tall.

"I'm hungry, Dave. How about you? We have been looking at prairie flowers and insects all morning."

"Right, let's eat!"

"Mike, this is a nice spot to eat. I hope Mom packed something good."

"Mm, this drink is good. What a great lunch. I'm full and ready to go."

"Dave, look at this orange flower. It's over here among all these black-eyed Susans. What do you think it is?"

"Wow, this is a **Turk's-cap lily**."

Most flowers smell sweet.

"Mike, what does the **_Turk's-cap lily_** smell like?"

"It has no smell to it. Look how the orange petals curl up and the flower hangs down. It looks like a hat."

The **Turk's-cap lily** has six flower petals that are orange with brown spots. There is a green star at the center of the flower. The leaves are found in whorls, or circles, along the stem. They grow three to six feet tall.

"Dave, look at the orange pollen all over my hand."

"Pollen is what sticks to the bees' legs, just like your hand, as they gather nectar to take back to the hive."

"The **Turk's-cap lily** sure is a pretty flower. It is different than the yellow coneflower and purple prairie clover plants we have seen."

Native Americans used the plant bulb of this lily to make soup.

"Mike, I see another reddish-orange flower that looks like a lily. But this one is different. This is a **wood lily**."

The petals stand straight up like a crown. The petals are small at the base and wide at the end. The stem is shorter than the Turk's-cap lily's stem and has narrow green leaves. They grow one to three feet tall.

"Mom says there are many different grasses on a prairie. Mike, come and look at this grass. It sure is tall. It is called **big bluestem**. It is the tallest grass on the prairie."

It grows three to ten feet tall. Some of the grasses are also short, like little bluestem, which grows two to four feet tall.

"Dave, Mom said **big bluestem** is also called turkey foot grass. This is because there are always three seed heads. The seed heads look like turkey feet. See my hand?"

The grass grows in bunches. American bison, or buffalo, grazed on this prairie grass.

"Mike, come look at this spider web. It is on **big bluestem** grass. I wonder where the spider is."

"How big do you think he is?"

"Look at this funny-looking plant that I found. It looks like it belongs in the desert, not on a prairie."

"Mike this is named **rattlesnake master**. The flowers are white and look like prickly balls and smell like honey."

The leaves are thin and have little teeth on the edges. Pioneers believed that tea made from the roots would heal rattlesnake bites, giving this plant its odd name. It grows three to four feet tall.

"Be quiet! Dave, look over there. Is that a bird? It looks like a small hummingbird getting nectar from that pink flower."

"Mike, that isn't a bird. Mom says this is a **hummingbird clearwing moth**. It is very colorful with all those stripes on its body and has a little tail like a lobster. It flies like a hummingbird."

The pink flower is ***bergamot***. It has pink tube-like petals on a big pink-green center. The flowers smell like oranges. Bees, butterflies, and clearwing hummingbird moths just love this plant. ***Bergamot*** will grow well in a butterfly garden.

Bergamot also has a square stem with jagged, shiny green leaves. Native Americans used the flowers to make tea. It grows two to three feet tall.

"Dave, I see more coneflowers, but with pink-purple petals and an orange middle."

"This plant is **purple coneflower**. Mom has many of these plants in her flower garden."

The petals stick out and do not droop down as far as the yellow coneflower. They grow two to three feet tall.

"Mike, look at all the bright orange flowers. What do you think they are?"

"Mom taught me this plant is ***butterfly weed***."

It is part of the milkweed family. The stems are hairy and the green leaves are in whorls or circles. They grow one to two feet tall.

The butterflies and bees get nectar and pollen from the flowers of the *butterfly weed*.

"Dave, don't you just love watching the honey bees at work. They go from flower to flower gathering nectar. Look at all the flowers they have to choose from."

The seed pods of the *butterfly weed* have silky floss that is used to stuff pillows and life jackets.

"Mike, this purple-blue flower smells sweet. Mom calls this flower **spiderwort**. It is different than any of the flowers we have looked at. I can't believe there are all these different-colored flowers on a prairie."

See how the **spiderwort** flowers are all bunched together to form a cluster. Each flower has only three petals. The leaves are thin and stick out around the flowers. Native Americans crushed the leaves and put them on insect bites or stings. They grow one to three feet tall.

"Mike, come look at what I've found. A bigger spider web than before! Look how it shines in the sunlight. I see the black spider in the center of its web. It's waiting for lunch."

"Dave, what a strange prairie plant! It has blue-purple flowers that look like tiny bottles. Mom told me this is called **bottle gentian**."

The flowers of the **bottle gentian** never open up. Large bumblebees are the only ones that can get nectar and pollen from this flower. The flowers are in circles around the stem of the plant. They grow six inches to two feet tall.

"Mike, we have found so many interesting prairie plants and insects today. All the flowers have such different names. But it is time to say goodbye to our prairie and go home."

"Dave, what an adventure! Maybe we can come back and explore another day. I just know there are many more plants and insects to see."

Printed in the United States
By Bookmasters